JOKES from the Back Seat 2

MORE **Humor for Kids!**

Includes "Hidden" Vault

JOKES

from the

Back Seat 2

MORE Humor for Kids!

Jokes, Riddles, Funny Cartoons, Tongue-Twisters,
Hilarious "Rokes & Jiddles," Science Jokes,
Sports Jokes, Puns, and Much More!

Includes "Hidden" Vault

JoBo

WALNUT STREET BOOKS

LANCASTER,
PENNSYLVANIA

Acknowledgments

Thanks to Steve, Lucinda, Titus, Linda, Marilyn, Will,
Bernardo, Adrian, Alex, Penn, Eric, Ruth, Luke, Anna, Clair,
Jim, Barb, Morgan, Dan and a long-enduring Marilyn.

Table of Contents

"*Honey, I think the mirror is malfunctioning again.*"

THREE IMPORTANT NOTES—
(<u>before</u> you read this book)

1. If you find a joke with a small "V" and a number, such as "V6," that indicates that you can go to "The VAULT" at the back of this book (the upside-down pages), beginning on page 126.

In The VAULT, you will find additional information about that joke, including what might make it funny. For example:

> Someone asked me to help check
> his balance at an ATM. So I
> pushed him over. v6

If you go The VAULT and look for V6, it will say:

V6 Balance means how much money you have in your account as well as how well you can stand up.

2. There are 6 pages in this book that you'll need to read with the help of a mirror.

These are pages 28 & 29, 74 & 75, and 110 & 111. Just hold them to a mirror to read!

3. Some pages are upside down. To read them, stand on your head!

Jokes

A mother sent her son to the corner store for a gallon of milk. She added, "If they have eggs, buy a dozen."

The boy returned with 12 gallons of milk.

I got an award for procrastination. I'll pick it up later. v1

Two kids meet on opposite sides of a river. One shouts to the other, "Help me get to the other side!"

The other kid replies, "You are on the other side!"

What did the horse wearing a sweater say to another horse?

"Won't you be my neigh-bor?"

Zach: "I drank so much milk yesterday it came out of my ears."

Emily: "Yeah, I saw, it was past your eyes!" v2

I didn't know how bad off I was until a person stole my identity, and it ruined his life.

To the guy who invented zero, thanks for nothing.

I ate so much bread that I became a roll model. v3

At Mr. Smith's funeral, Bob asked Mrs. Smith if he could say a word.

Mrs. Smith: Of course.

Bob: Plethora.

Mrs. Smith: Thank you, that means a lot. v4

A man goes into a barber shop with a frog on his head.

The barber said, "You have an unusual growth on you."

The frog replied, "I know, I touched a toad." v5

Johnny had such a big house that he would brag about it to friends.

One day he said to visiting Sally, "My yard is so big it takes me two hours to ride my bike around the edge."

To which Sally replied, "Yeah, I used to have a bike like that."

"*I think you're missing this.*"

A man goes into a café and orders three pieces of apple pie.

The waiter asks him why.

The man replies, "My two brothers moved out west, and I always eat a piece of pie for each of them, in addition to mine."

This goes on for a number of weeks, and one evening the man asks for two pieces of pie instead of three.

The waiter asks, "Did something happen to one of your brothers?"

The man replies, "No, I've just decided to stop eating pie."

I bought the world's worst thesaurus—not only is it terrible, it's terrible.

Sign in window:

> **TV for sale. $1. Unfortunately,**
> **the volume is stuck on high.**

I thought, "Well, I can't turn that down."

Someone asked me to help check his balance at an ATM. So I pushed him over. V6

I got an award for laziness but I don't think I'll bother to go pick it up.

A whole bunch of trout were queued up at the sports store checkout.

You don't often see fish in line. v7

My three favorite things are eating my football and not using commas. v8

If you can think of what you call a baby fish, let minnow. v9

If I got an award for the blankest wall, where would I put it?

I like to use big words that I don't know the meaning of. It makes me feel photosynthesis and retrograde. v10

I was driving by a restaurant that had a sign that read, "Breakfast served all day."

Although I was tempted, I realized I just didn't have time for that.

Og invented donuts but they didn't catch on till he started using dough instead of stone.

It's all
fun and games...

Perhaps you've heard someone warn you against too much roughhousing fun and horseplay by saying, "It's all fun and games till someone loses an eye."

They mean that the fun could get out of hand and someone could get hurt.

Here are some variations on that. See if you can figure out what changes in each example. Reading them out loud may increase the fun.

It's all fun and games tll someone loses an i.

It' all fun and game till omeone take all the s's.

It's all gun and fames till someone switches the letters.

At's ill gun and fames sill tomeone mitches swore letters.

It is all fun and games till someone removes the contraction.

It's all   and   till   takes all the nouns.

It's ll fn nd gms tll smn tks ll th vwls.

Its all fun and games till someone takes the apostrophe.

It's all fun and games till something gets
really really really small.

It's all fun and games till s0me0ne replaces the o's
with zer0es.

It's all fun and games till someone repeats themselves and it's all fun and games.

I's all fun and games ill someone drinks the t.

And now let's go a step further....

It's all bumpy roads and loose lug-nuts till someone
loses a tire.

It's all anger and annoyance till someone loses their
ire.

It's all playing and matches till someone looses a
fire.

"*Ear ache? That's nothing.
I have a sore throat.*"

Riddles

Q: What did the hat say to the scarf?

A: You hang around while I go on ahead.

Q: Can a grasshopper jump higher than the Washington Monument?

A: Of course, the Washington Monument can't jump at all.

Q: How can you tell if there's a whale in your refrigerator?

A: The door won't close.

Q: What gets bigger the more you take away?

A: A hole.

Q: What if everyone had a red car?

A: We'd be a red car nation.

Q: What do you call someone who speaks two languages?

A: Bilingual.

Q: What do you call someone who speaks three languages?

A: Trilingual.

Q: What do you call someone who speaks one language?

A: American. v11

Q: Why is there so much teasing in a sewing shop?

A: All the ribbon.

Q: What do you call an anxious carnivorous dinosaur?

A: A nervous Rex.

Q: What do you call a cow that's just white, not black and white?

A: A Halfstein. v12

Q: How do you get three hippos, four elephants, and a mouse in a car?

A: Put the hippos in the front seat, the elephants in the back seat, and the mouse in the glove compartment.

Q: What has a bed and a mouth, but doesn't sleep or talk?

A: A river.

Q: Whose skeleton is scattered all over Europe?

A: Napoleon Bonepart.

"Sure it's a swamp, but at least we don't live in France." v13

Q: What do you call an embarrassing fake father?

A: A faux pa. v14

Q: Why is Peter Pan always flying?

A: Because he never lands.

I like Peter Pan jokes because they never get old. v15

Q: What did the envelope say to the stamp?

A: Stick with me and we'll go places.

Q: What do you say to three holes in the ground?

A: Well, well, well.

Q: Why did the cow stand up straight?

A: She wanted to have good pasture.

Q: What did the hungry clock do?

A: Went back four seconds.

Q: How does the man on the moon cut his hair?

A: Eclipse it!

Q: What did the mayo say to the fridge?

A: Close the door, I'm dressing.

Q: What do you get when you drop a piano down a mine shaft?

A: A flat miner. V16

Q: Why haven't I been using my fireplace?

A: It has the flu(e). V17

Q: Why did the can crusher quit her job?

A: It was soda pressing.

Q: How do you keep your toes warm?

A: With a toaster.

Q: What's the difference between a birdwatcher and a train?

A: The birdwatcher says, "That's a swallow" and the train says, "Choo-choo." v18

Q: Why did the woman fall into the well?

A: Because she couldn't see that well.

Q: What do you call a father who stood in front of the light so that his son had trouble reading?

A: You can call him an eclipse—he blocked the light of the son.

Q: Is climate change melting the ice caps?

A: We'll sea.

(You need a mirror.)

Was it something I said?

(You need a mirror.)

Q: What do you call a dog that does magic tricks?

A: A labracadabrador.

Q: What do you call a seagull flying over the bay?

A: A bagel.

Q: What did the pirate say when he turned 80 years old?

A: Aye matey. v79

Q: How do you make a rock float?

A: Add two scoops of ice cream and a cherry.

Q: Why did the turkey join a band?

A: Because it had drumsticks.

Q: What has gray skin, four legs and a trunk?

A: A mouse on vacation.

Q: Why don't ducks tell jokes while flying?

A: They might quack up.

Q: What did one nut say to the other nut that she was chasing?

A: I'm a cashew. v20

Q: Why didn't French fries originate in France?

A: Because they were cooked in Greece.

Q: Why couldn't Lucy play a wind instrument?

A: Because she got a Flute shot.

Q: What do you call a burnt, hole-filled cheese?

A: Swiss charred. v21

Q: What is green and fuzzy, has four legs and, if it falls from a tree, it will kill you?

A: A pool table.

Q: What does Neil Armstrong say when no one laughs at his moon jokes?

A: Guess you had to be there.

Q: The Russet potato ask the orange potato, "Are you really a potato at all?"

A: It replied "Yes, I yam."

Q: How do you get 150 Canadians out of a swimming pool?

A: Calmly ask, "Could everyone please get out of the pool?"

"When should we tell him
he has to go back and put
in the hyperlinks?"

Q: How is church music distributed?

A: Through organ pipes.

Q: What time does Sean Connery arrive at Wimbledon?

A: Tennish. v22

Q: What's even worse than raining cats and dogs?

A: Hailing taxis.

Q: Why didn't Gregor ever get to be a monk?

A: He never got the chants.

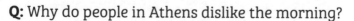

Q: What do you call someone who hangs out with musicians?

A: A drummer.

Q: Why do people in Athens dislike the morning?

A: Because dawn is tough on Greece.

Rhyming Reduplication

There are a number of words that are each made up of two words that rhyme. These "half-words" mean essentially nothing by themselves, but together have a meaning that usually sounds like the words when you say them.

Try matching these rhyming reduplications with their meanings. (Place the numbers in the correct blank.)

_____ **Zigzag**   1. dance

_____ **Higgledy piggledy**   2. flash to convince

_____ **Hodgepodge**   3. back and forth

_____ **Hokey pokey**   4. very good

_____ **Razzle-dazzle**   5. all confused
                                   and unorganized

_____ **Super-duper**   6. a mixture

(See V23 for the answers.)

Portmanteau

A "portmanteau" is a large trunk or suitcase, usually made of leather and opening into two equal parts.

So when you have two words that combine to make a new word, you can call it a "portmanteau" (pronounced—"port-man-tow").

In 2016, Britain's planned exit from the European Union became known as "Brexit."

"Microsoft" is a portmanteau of microcomputer and software.

"Amtrak" is a portmanteau of America and track. Without the "c"!

"Gerrymandering" is a combination of the man who famously carved up a voting district to his advantage, Governor Elbridge Gerry, and the shape the district looked like—a salamander.

"Velcro" is a portmanteau of the French words velours (velvet) and crochet (hook).

"Hassle" comes from haggle and tussle.

"Smog" comes from smoke and fog.

"Chortle" comes from chuckle and snort.

A "spork" is both spoon and fork.

A "skort" is part skirt and part shorts.

"Telethon" comes from telephone and marathon.

"Blog" comes from web and log.

"Medicare" comes from medical and care.

"Motel" comes from motor and hotel.

"Camcorder" comes from camera and recorder.

"Podcasting" comes from iPod and broadcasting.

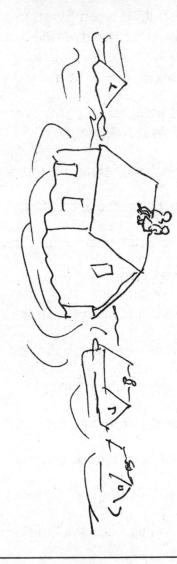

"Did you turn the TV off?"

More Jokes

Mountains are funny. In fact, they're hill areas.

My friend asked me: "What rhymes with flower?"
I said: "No, it doesn't."

My favorite time of day is 6:30, hands down!

1) You are reading this.
2) You are a smart kid.
3) You can't say the letter "K" without separating your lips.
4) You just tried to do it.
6) You are laughing at yourself.
7) You have a smile on your face and you skipped No. 5.
8) You just checked to see if there is a No. 5.
9) And you laughed at that, too.
10) And now you showed this to someone else.

My friend asked me to help him round up his 27 sheep. I said "30." V24

I will get an award for clairvoyance.

I signed up for a course on money management but my check bounced. I thought that would prove I needed the class.

A man was hiking in the Grand Canyon when a rattlesnake startled him.

He jumped into the air with fear and was found hanging on a branch 197 feet (60 meters) above the canyon floor.

The ranger asked how he managed to grab the branch so high in the air.

He said, "Well, to be honest, I missed it on the way up, but grabbed it on the way back down."

My teacher told me I had to stop acting like a flamingo. So I had to put my foot down.

I depend on my fingers. I can always count on them.

Q: What do we want?

A: Low flying airplane noises!

Q: When do we want them?

A: NNNEEEEEAAAAAOOOWWWWW!

"Another formal dinner?
Can't we ever go out
for fast food?"

Eric wanted to give his wife a dozen roses, but he hadn't botany. v25

I couldn't figure out why the baseball kept getting larger. Then it hit me.

I won a Sliver medal...but I got it out. v26

Young Billy was camping with his friend Steve. Steve told Billy he had no sense of direction. Billy got mad and packed up his tent and right.

I've been told I'm condescending.

(that means I talk down to people)

When I was young, I was so skinny that I had to run around in the shower to get wet.

Kid: Mom, what's a metaphor?

Mom: My life is a train wreck.

Kid: I know Mom, but what's a metaphor?

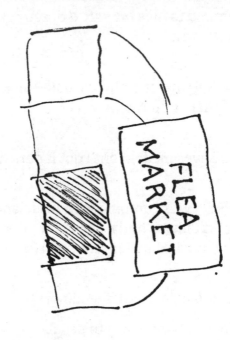

"But Mom, why does anyone want to buy fleas?"

MORE
Rhyming Reduplication

(See page 34 for explanation.)

____ **Boogie-woogie**	1. fancy
____ **Walkie-talkie**	2. messy
____ **Hoity-toity**	3. confused
____ **Wingding**	4. easy
____ **Ragtag**	5. portable radio
____ **Easy-peasy**	6. party
____ **Hurdy-gurdy**	7. instrumental blues
____ **Pell-mell**	8. instrument

(See V27 for the answers.)

These next few stories and sayings are called "Rokes and Jiddles." They should be read aloud. Try it.

Can you figure out the real story or saying behind what's printed here?

These are fun to read out loud to your friends and family. You may need to practice, because they can be tongue twisters. Give it a try!

The Rord of the Lings tells about a Frobbit named Hodo from Eiddle Marth who had a ragic ming. He mavelled to Trordor and restroyed the ding thy browing it into the drack of coom.

Wollum gas hot nappy.

Hary mad a little lamb, its weece flas snite as whow and therywhere what Wary ment the wamb las gure to so.

Mow huch cood would a choodchuck wuck if a coodchuck would wuck chood?

Sally sells seashells at the seashore.
(Well that didn't work well...)

Once ton a upime
There was a pandsome hrince
And a peautifil brincess...

The bruick quown jox fumped over the dazy log.

Weology is a gonderful stield to fudy. Finerals and mossils are always bun and feautiful.

In dry meams I fan cly, near the nound and grot foo tast.

To cix a fomputer ourn it tff and agurn ot in tain.

A nose by any other rame would swell as smeet.

Yow do hou det gown eff an olephant? Dou yon't, gou yet duwn off a dock.

Lurn teft, ren thight and ren thight again and ren thight again and bou're yack stere you wharted.

To take moast, blice some sread and top it in the poaster. Hush the pandle whown and den it oops put, knon't use a dife to get it out. PLULL THE PUG!

More Jokes

Where did Noah keep his elderly bees?

In the Ark hives!

Dry erase boards are remarkable.

A bank robber was caught by the police and put in a lineup.

When he was picked out, he objected, "How could they tell it was me? I had a mask on."

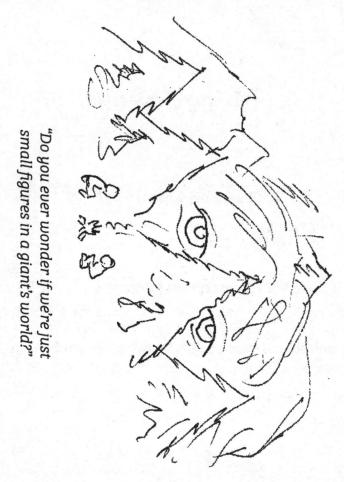

"Do you ever wonder if we're just small figures in a giant's world?"

What do you think? Will glass coffins become popular?

Remains to be seen!

Cinderella was a not a great soccer player. One problem was that she always ran away from the ball. Which is not surprising since her coach was a pumpkin.

Who wears the largest helmet on an ice hockey team? The one with the largest head.

An egotistical man built a massive building. His friend said, "Don't you think you're being a bit prideful, building such a big thing?"

"Ah, but I named it after you."

The friend was so honored that he told everyone he knew, until the day he saw the building, and there above the door it said, "After You."

Anna bought a new bow-and-arrow set, but it just didn't work very well. She looked in the user's manual and then she found the troubleshooting section. v28

Little Jimmy knew that he would have a tough time filling his father's shoes.

A writer once said, "People often accuse me of 'stealing other peoples' work' and being 'a plagiarist.'

"Their words, not mine..."

A driver asked a farmer on a country road for directions to the farm market.

He told her, "Go straight up the road till you reach the place where the barn burned down. Make a right where the old oak used to be, and then go on the dirt road till you see a barn with a horse out front, and then make another right and continue up a mile."

"What if the horse isn't out front?" the driver asked.

The farmer said, "Make a right anyway."

Daughter: "Mom, may I watch TV?"

Mom: "You can watch all you want, just don't turn it on."

Mrs. Eggplant to Miss Squash: "Meet my esteemed friend, Mr. Broccoli."

Mr. B: "To be honest, sometimes I'm stir-fried." v29

Tom Swifties

Tom Swifty jokes are named for Tom Swift, a fictional inventor created by Victor Appleton in the early 1900s. He was known for not liking to repeat "he said," so he added adverbs and modifiers instead.

One might say, for example, "I can run," said Tom quickly.

Or better yet, "I am fast," said Tom Swiftly.

Try reading these aloud and it will be easier to get the joke.

"I lost my hair!" said Tom baldly.

"Look at all those Navy ships!" said Tom fleetingly.

"Shall we go camping?" asked Tom intently. v30

"Let's eat at McDonalds!" said Tom archly.

"I think we're in Nebraska," Tom stated flatly.

"This knife isn't sharp," said Tom bluntly.

"What number could be between 7 and 9?" asked Tom considerately. v31

"Are you the host?" Tom guessed.

"I'm switching teams," Tom decided. v32

"I hate using zippers," Tom snapped.

"I'm not thinking of anything," said Tom thoughtlessly.

"I like to go parachuting," Tom explained. v33

"I like living by the nuclear reactor," said Tom glowingly.

"I'd like mustard and ketchup with that," said Tom with relish.

"We need a sign for the exit," Tom pointed out.

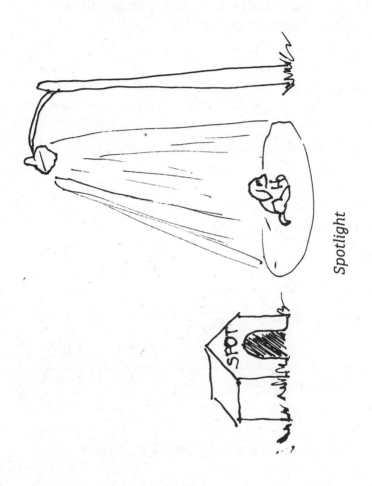

Spotlight

"Do you know what a bunch of lions is called?"
Tom asked with pride. V34

"I need more spice," said Tom sagely.

"That's not real," said Tom mockingly.

"That hippopotamus is selfish, mean, and ugly,"
said Tom hypocritically. V35

"I can read music," Tom noted.

"I think I have poison ivy," said Tom rashly.

"I'll put it together," Tom rejoined.

"Does anyone know our location?" Tom asked warily. V36

"How can we get water from here to there?" Tom piped.

"I heard they don't even have electricity down that street."

Quotes—with a Twist

The trouble with being punctual is that nobody is there to appreciate it.

—Franklin P. Jones

I did not attend his funeral, but I sent a nice letter saying I approved of it.

—Mark Twain

A lie gets halfway around the world before the truth has a chance to get its pants on.

—Winston S. Churchill

I like long walks, especially when they are taken by people who annoy me.

—Fred Allen

Get your facts first, then you can distort them as you please.

—Mark Twain

I get up every morning and read the obituary column. If my name's not there, I eat breakfast.

—George Burns

Clothes make the man. Naked people have little or no influence on society.

—Mark Twain

When I was a boy, the Dead Sea was only sick.

—George Burns

When I die, I want to die like my grandfather, who died peacefully in his sleep. Not screaming, like all the passengers in his car.

—Will Rogers

A committee is a group of the unprepared, appointed by the unwilling to do the unnecessary.

—Fred Allen

"I learned everything I know at my mother's knee or some other joint."

—Adlai Stevenson

Bonus words

Cattywampus

Ancient Romans would file off the corners of dice so they could cheat in gambling. They were called "Cater-trey" dice from an ancient term for four-cornered. This evolved into "catacorner" (or "kitty-corner") for diagonal, across from each other.

In the American South, the word "cattywampus" has meant the same, but its meaning was enlarged to mean "out of alignment" or "in disarray."

Use it in a sentence for the folks in the front seat, as in "All my books fell off the seat, and now everything is all cattywampus."

* * *

I once saw a trash truck that said "We refuse no refuse." V37

* * *

Think about these words and read the sentence out loud:

I used to wind my yarn till it was all wound up and then the wind would blow so hard that flying wood debris would wound me.

How many words are spelled the same and yet can sound differently? Did you read what I read?

* * *

I auto be better at spelling.

It says cheer that spelling is important. You don't want to be hanging around pool halls with acoustic in your hand.

Four example, ewe knead to have the cents to coin-cide when it reigns. And which way to turn adore knob. Or how to put debate on a fishing hook.

You might get a job cleaning chimneys if it soots you. And if you know how to reed, you can choose a hotel wisely or you might end up in a violin. V38

"Mommy! Surmise what!
Surmise what! We learned a new
word in school today, can you
surmise what it might be?"

What words spell another word if read backwards? Like —

draw = ward

Dessert = ?

Deliver = ?

Straw = ?

What words like these can you think of?

_____ = _____

_____ = _____

_____ = _____

* * *

Here's a nice old word we don't use much anymore—

Wamble

It means—to move unsteadily.

So when you hop out of the car and your legs need to stretch, you can say to your parents, "Hey, watch me wamble over to the rest stop."

He was an it till he tried to quit and found there is no exit.

*   *   *

Buffalo buffalo buffalo—three meanings?

The buffalo was buffaloed into going to Buffalo.

*   *   *

Q: What do "abstemiously" and "facetiously" have in common?

A: They each use all the vowels. V39

*   *   *

There is a story about four people: Everybody, Somebody, Anybody, and Nobody.

There was an important job to be done, and Everybody was sure that Somebody would do it. Anybody could have done it, but Nobody did it. Somebody got angry about that because it was Everybody's job.

Everybody thought Anybody could do it, but Nobody realized that Everybody wouldn't do it. Everybody blamed Somebody, when actually Nobody asked Anybody.

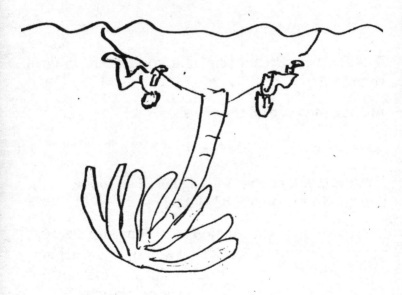

"Do you worry about the
sea level rising?"

MORE
Rhyming Reduplication

(See page 34 for explanation.)

____ **Claptrap**		1. commotion
____ **Kowtow**		2. haphazard
____ **Jiggery-pokery**		3. nonsense
____ **Hubbub**		4. mischief
____ **Harum-scarum**		5. bow to
____ **Teeny-weeny**		6. impress with flash, divert attention
____ **Hocus-pocus**		7. small
____ **Willy-nilly**		8. unorganized

(See V40 for the answers.)

Favorite Old Jokes

Teacher: Name two pronouns.

Student: Who, me?

You can't RUN through a campsite. You can only RAN, because it is past tents.

Sally: I never argue with unreasonable people.

Bob: That's dumb.

Sally: I agree with you.

What I if told you that

you read the first line wrong?

I have not yet begun to procrastinate. v41

I'm confused. No, wait—maybe I'm not.

At age 20, we worry about what others think of us.

At age 40, we don't care what others think about us.

At age 60, we discover they haven't been thinking about us at all!

Kansas: 2 million years tsunami free! v42

I had a job at an orange juice factory but I got canned because I couldn't concentrate.

"I prefer to think of myself as black with white stripes rather than white with black stripes."

A sign said the used psychology book was $3.50.

I gave the cashier a $5 bill.

The cashier coughed and $1.50 came out of his mouth.

So it's true—I've been told that change comes only from within...

The donut doctor practices holistic medicine.

Did you hear about the man who was built upside-down?

His nose ran and his feet smelled.

How does a psychic pay for school?

In tuition.

My horse, Mayo, makes tuna salad for the whole family and never complains. Well, sometimes Mayo neighs.

(You need a mirror.)

"I have plenty right here
in these boxes."

(You need a mirror.)

It was so hot Anna couldn't get the eggs home from the store before they were hard boiled.

Are tailors the best for fitting a suit?

So it seems. v43

The brass ensemble disbanded.

Jimmy wasn't feeling well, but he wanted to go to the playground anyway.

Before Jimmy went on the slide he covered his body in lard.

After that, he went downhill fast.

My sister's laptop broke. So, to cheer her up, I went out and got her an identical one.

She was SO mad. She said, "What am I going to do with two broken laptops?"

 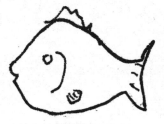

"I find fish to be so gillable." v44

What do you get when you pour warm water down a rabbit hole?

Hot cross bunnies.

What do you get when you cross a deer and a wolf?

A wolf.

Accordion player Bob: Did you hear my last recital?

Sally: I certainly hope so.

What did the maple tree (who was in a bad mood) say to the oak tree?

Leaf me alone.

I stayed up all night wondering when the sun would come up and then it dawned on me.

What is illegal?

A sick bird.

A farmer won a contest for his farm equipment. It was an amateur tractor, not a pro tractor. v45

Farmer 1: "The veterinarian still hasn't arrived at the dairy!"

Farmer 2: "Don't have a cow."

Can you lose money by gambling?

You bet you can.

If a cow doesn't produce milk, is it called a "milk dud" or an "udder failure"?

Science Jokes

Orion is an average constellation. I give it just three stars. v46

Q: What kind of tree fits in your hand?

A: A palm tree.

Q: Why do bees have sticky hair?

A: They use honeycombs.

The hungry black hole had a light lunch. v47

Q: Do physicists study dark energy?
A: It doesn't matter.

There are 3 kinds of people in the world...those who are good at math, and those who aren't! v48

There are two kinds of people. Those who understand binary and those who don't. v49

Bad jokes make me numb, but bad math jokes make me number.

It's always good to have a mathematician at a meeting. They know how to sum up.

Why did the dinosaur cross the road?

Because the chicken wasn't around yet.

There are two kinds of people. Those who can ex-trapolate. v50

The Earth's rotation really makes my day.

Q: What are moving left to right, right now?

A: Your eyes.

Parallel-line lovers are destined never to meet. v51

Q: Did you hear about the mathematician who was afraid of negative numbers?

A: He'd stop at nothing to avoid them.

A meteorologist tried to pinpoint when the fog would roll in, but he mist.

What do trees swim in?

Their trunks.

I have a scientist friend who only lets you knock on his door. He wants the no-bell prize.

Never loan a geologist money. They think a short time is a million years.

If there's an earthquake, whose fault is it?

If you buy a proton and an electron, you get a neutron, free of charge!

Q: What place are you in if you pass the person who is second place in a race?

A: Second place.

There's a fine line between a numerator and a denominator.

I always read about gravity. I'm attracted to it.

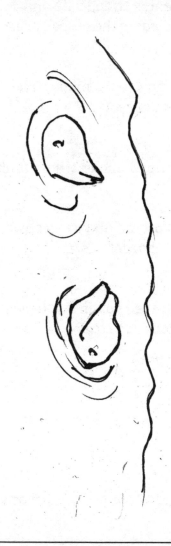

"You give me porpoise in life."

I read about black holes everywhere. You just can't escape them.

In cell biology, multiplication and division are the same. V52

No matter how well you planet, it's hard to throw a party that includes the entire solar system. Everyone just circles the sun.

The optimist sees the glass half full. The pessimist sees the glass half empty. The chemist sees the glass completely full: half of it with liquid and half with air.

Why didn't the quantum particle cross the road?

It was already on both sides. V53

What's a nuclear physicist's favorite food?

Fission Chips. V54

"I'll believe anything,
I'm so gullible."

Sports Jokes

Why is it windy at a sporting event?

All the fans.

I'm not good at most sports, but bowling is right up my alley.

Which baseball player holds water?

The pitcher.

Why does a pitcher raise one leg when she throws?

If she raised both legs, she'd fall down.

I knew my friend was a soccer referee when he sent me a yellow card for Christmas.

The golfer had to change his socks because he had a hole in one.

I couldn't sleep because, just outside my window, a tennis player was raising a racquet.

Q: What did the soccer announcer yell when a ball hit a bird at the seashore?
A: Guuuuuuuullllllllllllllllllllllllllll!

The basketball player grabbed a chicken on the basketball court. He had been looking for a fowl. v55

The hardest part of skydiving is the ground.

Q: Which animal is best at baseball?
A: A bat.

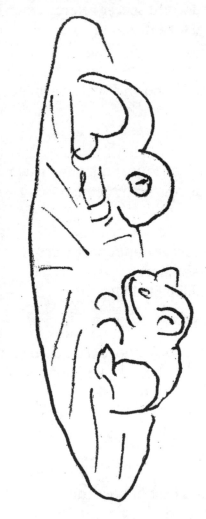

"Did you hear that Bob croaked last night?"

More Rokes & Jiddles

(Can you switch some of the letters and figure out these sayings? Answers are upside down.)

A mool and his foney are poon sarted.

A fool and his money are soon parted.

A wad borkman tames his blools.

A bad workman blames his tools.

A hird in the band is worth bwo in the tush.

A bird in the hand is worth two in the bush.

A mog is a dan's fest briend.

A dog is a man's best friend.

A senny paved is a eenny parned.

A penny saved is a penny earned.

A wicture is porth a wousand thords.

A picture is worth a thousand words.

A tising ride bifts all loats.

A rising tide lifts all boats.

A stolling rone mathers no goss.

A rolling stone gathers no moss.

A titch in stime naves sine.

A stitch in time saves nine.

A patched wot bever noils.

A watched pot never boils.

All dands on heck.

All hands on deck.

All loads read to Rome.

All roads lead to Rome.

All glat thitters is got nold.

All that glitters is not gold.

Good cings thome to wose who thait.

Good things come to those who wait.

All pings must thass.

All things must pass.

All plork and no way jakes Mack a bull doy.

All work and no play makes Jack a dull boy.

All you leed is nove.

All you need is love.

All is bor the fest in the best of all wossible porlds.

All is for the best in the best of all possible worlds.

Letter bate nan thever.

Better late than never.

Setter bafe san thorry.

Better safe than sorry.

Geware of breeks gearing bifts

Beware of Greeks bearing gifts.

Fig bish eat fittle lish.

Big fish eat little fish.

Hold cands, harm weart.

Cold hands, warm heart.

Do bot nite the thand hat yeeds fou.

Do not bite the hand that feeds you.

Do lot nook a hift gorse in me thouth.

Do not look a gift horse in the mouth.

It vakes a tillage to chaise a rild.

It takes a village to raise a child.

Flime ties.

Time flies.

Mime is toney.

Time is money.

A stolling rone mathers no goss.

A rolling stone gathers no moss.

More Jokes

David was doing well till someone stole his ID. Now he's just Dav.

When a swarm of birds descended on her property, the owner put metal casings around each of the trees. She wanted her yard to be impeccable.

Colonial Minute Men were notorious for avoiding British sympathizers. V56

I sold my boomerang 16 times.

"Do you think anyone delivers here?"

It's traditional to wish an actor well by saying, "Break a leg." That's because every play has a cast.

Q: Where are satises made?
A: In a satisfactory.

Q: What did 3 say to 5?
A: Have we metaphor?

Q: Why can't you take a kleptomaniac to a bookstore?
A: They take things literally.
Q: Why can't you take them to a beach?
A: They take things littorally. v57

A thief broke into my house last night and started searching for money. I woke up and searched *with* him.

My brother always throws socks at me, so I went away. I think he misses me, but he is getting closer.

Henry: Doc, it hurts when I poke my leg, and it hurts when I press my arm, and it hurts when I touch my face.

Doc: You have a broken finger.

Can you read this message?

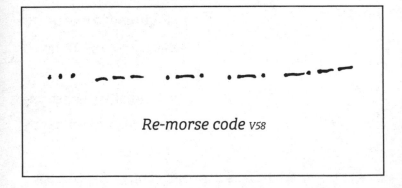

Re-morse code v58

Ireland has amazing growth. Its capital is Dublin.

A special store for those who failed arithmetic had a "buy two, get one" sale.

Spaghetti dances at meat balls.

Q: In what do you pack your food for a trip to Mexico?

A: Suitquesadilla.

Q: What do you call back-up Mexican food?

A: Just in quesadilla.

Q: What public service announcement would Mr. Spock make?

A: "Kids, don't play with superglue."

If life gives you melons, you're good at anagrams. (Hint: make lemonade!) v59

I bought my friend an elephant for his room.
He said, "Thank you."

I said, "Don't mention it." V60

I went to join the ambidextrous society tonight. But it didn't feel right, so I left. V61

Do you know any jokes about sodium?

Na. V62

I got second place in vacation homes. V63

A linguistics professor said that, "In English, a double negative forms a positive, but a double positive is never a negative."

But then a student said, "Yeah, right."

When people asked my grandfather how he was, he would reply, "Parts of me are excellent."

Becky ran into a concert hall and loudly said, "I'd like a hamburger and fries!"

The usher said, "This is a concert hall."

Becky lowered her voice, "I'd like a hamburger and fries."

On a train trip across the country, the passengers were alarmed when the train engine suddenly went silent.

The conductor announced, "I have bad news and good news. The bad news is the engine has stopped working. The good news is that we weren't cruising at 30,000 feet."

The lead goose yelled back at the rest, "If you want to pass, go ahead! I'm tired of all the honking!"

I came very close to all the right answers during the exam today. I was only two seats away.

A surgeon quickly drinks his milk in forceps.

Music jokes

Fur matta . . . . .and a bald matta

The musician always kept her bowls and silverware on the cadenza. V64

Sailors love concertmasters because they can always find the C.

Why was the pacifist uncomfortable at the orchestra?

He didn't like violins.

He played the same four pieces loudly 10 times.

It was forte.

Beethoven's favorite fruit?

Ba na na naaaaa.

Bassoon . . . . and Bass late

Old Favorites

In 1908, I. and M. Ottenheimer of Baltimore, MD, published a tiny paperback called, "New Jokes."

Here are some of them, modified to be less offensive. Why do think we don't find them as funny?

A boy went to a museum where he saw the skeleton of the King of Alzabatha. Next to it was a smaller skeleton, labeled "skeleton of King of Alzabatha as a boy."

Snoring is sheet music.

"Could I sell you an encyclopedia?"

"No, I wouldn't know how to ride it."

Every time I get on a ferry boat it makes me cross.

Jennifer: "Did you take a bath?"

Jon: "Why, is one missing?"

"My Christmas stocking had nothing in it."

"Mine did—a hole."

"How's your cold?"

"My cold is fine. I feel awful."

"What do you suppose Big Herman the neighborhood butcher weighs?"

"Meat."

Most things go to the buyer but coal goes to the cellar. V65

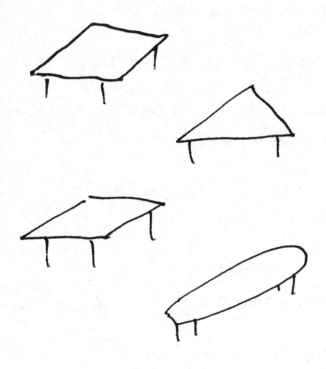

Tables King Arthur tried before discovering pi. V54

Advanced Science Jokes

Angular momentum—it's what makes the world go round. V66

When Heisenberg was stopped for speeding, the officer asked, "Do you know how fast you were going?"

He replied, "No, but I know where I am." V67

Q: How can you tell the difference between a chemist and a plumber?

A: Ask them to pronounce "unionized." V68

(You need a mirror.)

Helium walked into a restaurant. The bartender said, "We don't serve noble gasses in here." Helium didn't react. v69

An opinion without 3.1416 is just an onion. v70

What did the geometry teacher put on the sign when the cook took the pan down from the top shelf?

High pot in use. v71

I read a book about helium. I couldn't put it down. v72

It's all cycles and frequencies till someone gets Hertz. v73

I was going to tell you a time travel joke but you didn't get it.

(You need a mirror.)

—Something to think about

Consider the cicada. It burrows underground and emerges after years of hibernating.

Depending on the type, it re-emerges every year, or every 13 years, or every 17 years.

1,13,17. All prime numbers. How does a cicada know it's been 17 years? Why prime numbers? And why do they have to be so darn noisy?!

"You know Og and Mog have
Fire 2.0. It can burn whole logs." VTA

Jokes for the Front Seat

Here are some jokes you can try out on the people in the front seat.

What do you get when you combine a joke with a rhetorical question? V75

Why didn't Alexander make it big with the Bolshoi? He wasn't Godunov. V76

To gym instructor: "Can you teach me to do splits?"

"How flexible are you?"

"I can't make Tuesdays."

Four fonts walk into a restaurant and the waiter says, "We don't serve your type."

How can you tell when a singer is at your door?

They can't find the key and never know when to come in.

The odd oak tree had a lot of Quercus. v77

My name is Bond, Ionic Bond.

Taken not shared. v78

How many eye doctors does it take to change a lightbulb?

Is it one or two? One... or two?

So this classics professor goes to a tailor to get his pants mended. The tailor asks: "Euripides?" The professor replies "Yes. Eumenides?" v79

Q: Do you remember the name Quasimodo?

A: It rings a bell. v80

Q: What's the potential for a Superman remake?

A: It's looking up.

Q: What do we want?"

A: Autonomy!

Q: When do we want it?

A: Whenever you say it's okay. v81

Don't invite Nebuchadnezzar to a party. All he'll do is Babylon. v82

A family met at the mall and decided they'd meet later for dinner. The mother said, "Let's all meet back here in about $500."

A doctor told his ailing patient, "I'm sorry, you only have 10 left."

The patient asked, "Ten what? Years, Months? Weeks?"

The doctor replied, "9...8...7..."

Q: What does the Australian vacationing in Yellowstone wash her hands in?

A: A bison...

A woman was stopped for speeding. The police officer said, "It says here you need glasses to drive. Where are your glasses?"

She said, "I have contacts."

The officer said, "I won't be influenced! Now, where are your glasses?"

Bonus:
More Rokes & Jiddles

(See page 46 for instructions.)

Hork ward. Beam drig.

Go it soes.

Che the bange wou yish to wee in the sorld.

Fry and tail, nut bever tail to fry.

To lucceed in sife, nou yeed tho twings: cnorance and igonfidence.

All feneralizations are galse.

Plere's no thace hike lome.

Bife is letter smen you're whiling.

Biends are frorn, mot nade.

Moo tuch of a thood ging.

The muth is trore important fan the thacts.

A mog is a dan's frest biend.

Track of all jades—naster of mone.

V73 Hertz means cycles/per second, or how fast something is oscillating. It also sounds like hurts.

V74 Software often has versions like 1.0, 2.0, 2.1, etc., with each new version adding new features.

V75 This is itself a rhetorical question AND a joke! I think it's funny. Many people disagree with me.

V76 Alexander Godunov was a famous Russian ballet dancer. Godunov sounds like "good enough."

V77 Quercus is the genus of oak trees, as in *Quercus alba*, or white oak. It sounds kind of like "quirks."

V78 James Bond, 007, would say, "Bond, James Bond," and "shaken, not stirred." Ionic bonds take an electron rather than sharing them.

V79 Euripides was a Greek playright and Eumenides a Greek play. They sound like "you rippa these" and "you menda these."

V80 Quasimodo was a bell-ringing character in Victor Hugo's *Hunchback of Notre Dame*.

V81 Autonomy means complete independence, therefore, you wouldn't ask for someone else to approve when you ask for it.

V82 Nebuchadnezzar was the king of Babylon (which sounds like babble on). And what a great name! Do you think he was called Nebbie for short? Maybe only once...

V62 The chemical symbol for sodium is Na.

V63 Usually a vacation home is a second home that wealthy people have. So it's a second place.

V64 A credenza is a side table in a dining room. A cadenza is a solo part.

V65 In days gone by, people stored coal in their cellars to burn in their furnace for heat. Cellar sounds like seller.

V66 How a body rotates is defined by its angular momentum. So it makes the world go round.

V67 Heisenberg had a famous theory that said you can't know both location and speed of a particle. You can only observe one at a time.

V68 Plumbers belong to unions. Chemists deal with ions. Chemists might say un-ionized.

V69 Helium is a lighter-than-air element that does not react with other elements (something we call a noble gas). For example, it does not burn.

V70 pi = 3.1416... It's a wonderful and very useful number, and infinitely long.

V71 A hypotenuse is the side of a triangle that is opposite a right angle.

C ← hypotenuse

A

B

$$A^2 + B^2 = C^2$$

V72 See V69. It keeps rising.

V56 Notorious sounds like "No Tory." Tories were British sympathizers in the Revolutionary War.

V57 A kleptomaniac is someone who just can't help stealing things. Literally, means that's exactly what they'll do. But the second part of the joke is a coastal geology joke (and those jokes are rare). Littoral means "along the shore."

V58 Morse code is a series of dots and dashes. Use the chart below to see what the message says. And by the way, remorse means you are sorry.

V59 Melon is an anagram for lemon.

V60 The saying "There's an elephant in the room" means there's some big issue that everyone is ignoring. In this case, an elephant!

V61 Ambidextrous means you can use both your right and left hands equally.

V44 Gullible.

V45 There is no such thing as a professional tractor as opposed to an amateur one. But it sounds like protractor, a device for measuring angles.

V46 Orion is a constellation that has three stars in a line. One of them may be going supernova…

V47 Black holes are extremely dense with so much mass that they even pull light into their gravitational field, so no light escapes.

V48 This lists only two! Bad math.

V49 Binary means 1 and 0, or only two possible answers. So someone who sees things in a binary way sees everything in black and white, so to speak.

V50 Extrapolate means to estimate from past experience or extend a graph. When you read the sentence, you naturally want to add "and those who don't," which is an extrapolation.

V51 Parallel lines can never cross each other.

V52 In math multiplication and division are opposite concepts, but in biology, a cell divides in order to make more (multiply).

V53 Quantum particles are thought to sometimes be in two places at once.

V54 Fish and chips. (Fission is splitting an atom.)

V55 Fowl (a bird) sounds like foul.

V34 A group of lions is called a pride. Names for some other groups are—

- Bats: a colony
- Bees: a swarm
- Crows: a murder
- Eagles: a convocation
- Elephants: a parade
- Ferrets: a business
- Fish: a school
- Frogs: an army
- Geese: a gaggle
- Hippopotami: a bloat
- Lemurs: a conspiracy
- Parrots: a pandemonium
- Rabbits: a herd
- Whales: a pod
- Zebras: a zeal

V35 In my view, this is the best Tom Swifty here. Hippo – critical.

V36 Warily means cautiously. It sounds like where. Where-ily.

V37 This was actually written on a garbage truck in Tuscaloosa, Alabama. I saw it in 1973 and always admired the wit. Refuse (ree-'fuuz) means to reject and refuse ('ref-uuz) means trash.

V38 Vile inn.

V39 Abstentious means to be willing to hold back, or do without, while facetious means treating a serious subject with inappropriate humor. And they use all vowels, in alphabetical order.

V40 3,5,4,1,8,7,6,2.

V41 By not doing something you are surely procrastinating.

V42 A tsunami is a large wave caused by an undersea earthquake or slump. Kansas is so far inland that a wave would never reach that far.

V43 I'm proud of this joke. It makes a play on the sounds. "Sew it seams" sounding like "so it seems." It's not often you get two puns in one sentence.

V21 Swiss chard is a vegetable.

V22 Sean Connery is a Scottish actor famous for an accent that uses "ish" for "s." Ten-ish means about 10. Wimbledon is the famous tennis court in England.

V23 3,5,6,1,2,4.

V24 To round up means to use a round number to the nearest 10 above it. For example, you would round up 17 to 20.

V25 Botany (study of plants) sounds like "bought any."

V26 Sliver (like a splinter) sounds like silver.

V27 7,5,1,6,2,4,8,3.

V28 She had trouble shooting and used the troubleshooting (how to fix problems) manual.

V29 Esteemed sounds like "steamed" (versus stir-fried).

V30 Camp "in a tent."

V31 Consider – 8 – ly.

V32 De-sided.

V33 Explain = Ex means "out of," "plain" sounds like "plane." Out of the plane.

V8 Look what happens when you leave out commas! Instead of eating, my football, and not using commas, it becomes "eating my football."

V9 Minnow (meh no) is a baby fish. It sounds like "me know."

V10 The boy likes to use words he doesn't understand. So he uses photosynthesis and retrograde, two words that have nothing to do with how you feel. Photosynthesis is how plants convert sunlight, carbon dioxide, and water into sugars and oxygen. Retrograde means to go backwards.

V11 Because citizens of the US tend to spend much their lives speaking only one language, unlike much of the rest of the world.

V12 Versus a Holstein cow, which is black and white.

V13 French cuisine sometimes includes frog legs.

V14 "Faux" in French means "false." A *faux pas* ("fo paw") is French for "false step" or a social blunder.

V15 Peter Pan lives in Neverland and never grows old.

V16 A flat minor.

V17 Flue (inside of a chimney) sounds like flu (a virus).

V18 Swallow food and chew chew.

V19 I'm eighty.

V20 Catch you.

The Vault

V1 To procrastinate means to put off till later. (As my mother would say, "Tomorrow, tomorrow, not today, that's what lazy people say.") So if you got an award for doing that, you would pick it up later.

V2 "Past your eyes" sounds like pasteurize (to heat milk to eliminate harmful bacteria).

V3 Roll sounds like role.

V4 Plethora means a lot, as in "There are a plethora of jokes in this book."

V5 Usually people are worried that if they touch a toad they'll get a wart (you don't.) In this case, the frog touched a toad and grew a whole person!

V6 Balance means how much money you have in your account as well as how well you can stand up.

V7 "Fish in line" sounds like "fishing line." Queued means lined up.

About the Author

JoBo is the stage name of the funnyman and humorist who put this second book together. He also drew the cartoons and illustrations.

In real life, his name is Jay B. Parrish, a geophysicist by profession. (To find out where the name "JoBo" came from, check the back of his first book.)

Jay, enjoys jokes and riddles with his wife Marilyn, his children, and especially with his young grandchildren.

If you would like him to speak to your group, or if you have a joke to share with him for his next book, write to JoBo at Jobojokes@gmail.com.

Also by JoBo!

*Available wherever books are sold.
They make great gifts!*